The Unremarkable Death of Marilyn Monroe

A play in one act
by Elton Townend Jones

SERVING THEATRE

SF

SINCE 1830

WWW.SAMUELFRENCH.CO.UK
WWW.SAMUELFRENCH.COM

ISBN 978-0-57313203-2

www.samuelfrench.co.uk
www.samuelfrench.com

FOR AMATEUR PRODUCTION ENQUIRIES

UNITED KINGDOM AND WORLD EXCLUDING NORTH AMERICA
plays@SamuelFrench-London.co.uk
020 7255 4302/01

UNITED STATES AND CANADA
info@SamuelFrench.com
1-866-598-8449

Each title is subject to availability from Samuel French, depending upon country of performance.

Author's note

Marilyn Monroe was once the most famous movie star in the world; but maybe she was famous for all the wrong reasons: her image, her sex appeal, her frailties and failings. She was known for playing dumb blondes, for her love affairs, her increasing lateness on set and her drug dependency. When she suddenly died, one night in August 1962, she was only thirty-six years old. Posthumously, she became remembered for yet more wrong reasons: she was killed by the Kennedys, she was killed by the Mafia; she killed herself. The sensation over her death has managed, for a long time, to eclipse the sensation of her life and the last fifty years has seen her remembered for a plethora of things, the very least of which seems to be the woman herself.

I first fell for Marilyn when I was twelve – twenty years after her death – which means that I've known for thirty years that I wanted to produce a work that recognised and investigated the truth behind the make-up and the peroxide to reveal something more substantial than a mere footnote in the Kennedy story or a regurgitation of all those things we think we know about this fascinating and beguiling woman.

This was my original Dyad Productions pitch (which I later used in press and publicity copy):

Marilyn as we've never seen her before. Alone in her bedroom in dressing gown and slippers; no glitz, no glamour, no masks. Overdosed on pills, the woman behind the icon drifts back through her life via the memories of her closest relationships. Making a stark confessional to the physical embodiment of her fame, and repeatedly stalked by her own death, Marilyn tells all (DiMaggio, Gable, Miller; it's all here). Revealing her biting intelligence and an imperfect body, she exposes the truth behind the legend, leading us – in real time – to the very moment of her demise.

In researching this work, I made it my duty to only rely on information and anecdotes that came from multiple sources (unless it threw the corroborated facts into a kind of sharp relief that offered intriguing new glimpses of the real woman). Her life is documented in a thousand books, but her early years are often confused over the how and when of pivotal moments, and this is also true of her final hours. Regarding both, I have applied Occam's Razor. Of her demise, I have concluded that there was no conspiracy. There is nothing remarkable about her death. It was a tragic accident. That said, the play remains deliberately coy about this, allowing for future revelations on the matter.

Once I'd drawn my conclusions about Marilyn's death, my examination of her life – using books, watching newsreels and TV interviews, reading magazines and just spending long, long hours looking at photographs and imagining what she was thinking – led me to what I can only call my own 'Theory of Marilyn'. It is this theory that informs the 'plot' of the play, and I arrived at it by joining a few seemingly un-joined dots that would tie some of her earliest experiences to her final ones whilst also answering some questions about the most controversial aspects of her adult life.

So. What if Marilyn – or, as she knew herself, Noodle – were able to reflect upon her remarkable life, one final time in that hour before she faded from the world? And what if we were summoned there by her vivacious spirit to bear witness to her final testimony? Which Marilyn would we see? We'd see the real deal – a talented artist, a brilliant comedian, a frustrated intellectual; an attractive, loving woman afflicted with physical and mental conditions that cursed her working and emotional life. We'd get the how and when, but also the why of Marilyn. And a little more besides.

After all, as much as the play uses Marilyn and Hollywood as its medium, it is primarily an examination of love and relationships. There's no point in using quotes from the piece and ascribing them to Marilyn – she never said any of this. When she talks about love and sex and relationships, that's me talking. That's my own soul leaking. But since I was twelve, I've felt an affinity with the Noodle. I think we might agree on much when it comes to matters of the heart. And I'm certain that those reading and performing this play (whether in whole or in part) will find something of their own emotional experience here. You don't have to look or sound like Marilyn to feel this stuff. Noodle would be the first to tell you that.

Well, here she is: no bells, no whistles, the real Marilyn Monroe (if such a creation can be said to be real). Following rave reviews at Edinburgh 2013, the play has toured the UK and Ireland successfully throughout 2014-15, including short runs at Greenwich Theatre and St James' Theatre. Many thousands of people have now met the real Noodle. I hope I've done her memory justice and allowed us to better understand and appreciate the talent and vivacity we lost in August 1962. But never forget: despite my best intentions, the woman herself is capable of lying. And so is her writer. This is, after all, a work of fiction.

Elton Townend Jones

ELTON TOWNEND JONES

Elton wrote, directed and performed his first play aged 18, whilst studying Performing Arts in East Anglia, after which he spent five hungry years as a professional stage and TV actor. He subsequently gained a BA in Literature with Philosophy and ran a popular regional theatre. After writing and directing the short film '*Dear Eve...*', and penning *Cutting the Cord* at Battersea Arts Centre, he co-founded Dyad Productions with creative partner Rebecca Vaughan. To date, he has produced seven international touring hits, including *Austen's Women*, and *I, Elizabeth*. Of the others, he script-edited *Female Gothic*, wrote and acted in *The Diaries of Adam and Eve*, directed and script-edited *Christmas Gothic*, and wrote and directed *Dalloway* and *The Unremarkable Death of Marilyn Monroe*. Forthcoming writer/director projects would appear to include: *Jane Eyre - An Autobiography*, *The Time Machine*, *Lennon*, *Tristram Shandy* and *Bela Lugosi's Not Dead*. Outside Dyad, he writes prose fiction (notably two works for charity based on his beloved *Doctor Who*) and, as a freelance journalist, writes about music, television, books, theatre and film. He describes himself as a fabulist and magician.

You can find out more about Elton and keep up with his work at
www.dyadproductions.com

ACKNOWLEDGEMENTS

This play might at first glance seem to be about Marilyn Monroe, but really it's a play about love and the events in our lives that make us who we are. It couldn't exist without the kindness of the following: the truly legendary Rebecca Vaughan who made it happen and continues to make brilliant things happen; Waen Shepherd (my oldest, dearest mucker, who went beyond the call of duty, for which I'll always be grateful); everyone at Dyad Productions (Martin, Kate, Donna, Ben, Holly, Penny, and Mags); Vivian Smith, Wayne & Diane Townend, Arthur Edwards, and Walter Lindley (for a childhood full of words and magic); Frank Brown, Elliot Ray, Chris Mellor and the late, great Anita Kitchener (for believing in me when no-one else did); Andrew Coppin and Jo Richardson (for coming with me at the start); Guy and Sachi (for a leg-up); Alison, Lee, Timothy, Sarah, Matthew, Marina, Alan, Alys, and Glen (for always turning up); John Guilor and Stephen Russell (for keeping me going in the dark times); Dale and Leyton (for being the best brothers ever!); Jean & Dennis Townend (for always providing an escape); Kevin & Marion (for more than words can say); David Waters; the Murtons and Claude's; Marc Tompkins at Artisan; Gusto Edinburgh; all at Assembly; Felicity, Sarah and Emma at Samuel French; and the noodliest noodle of them all: Lizzie Wort, who was always utterly remarkable.

For Michael Smith and Derek Watson, who went too soon and whose unstinting love and support is dearly missed.

The Unremarkable Death of Marilyn Monroe was first performed as part of the Edinburgh Festival Fringe at Assembly Three, George Square, Edinburgh, on 1 August 2013, with the following cast:

NOODLE – Lizzie Wort

Directed by Elton Townend Jones
Designed by Elton Townend Jones
Lighting by Martin Tucker
Special Sounds by Waen Shepherd
Produced by Rebecca Vaughan, with Elton Townend Jones

A Dyad Production

MUSIC USE NOTE

NOTES FOR A PRODUCTION

It is Saturday, 4ʰ August 1962, 12305 Fifth Helena Drive, Brentwood, California. A warm, perhaps muggy evening, about 8pm. We are in the bedroom of Noodle, alias Marilyn Monroe.

THE BEDROOM

Sparse, plain and shabby. Unglamorous, crushingly normal, a mess. Unfinished, no formal ornamentation.

A bed: small divan, single, unmade. Simple white sheets, nothing fancy, white pillows, silver shiny comforter. Angled so the end of the bed is toward the audience at downstage centre, the head of the bed being upstage right.

Small bedside table/nightstand with lamp, plus several cosmetic and pill bottles. Stage right.

A bedroom chair, maybe Lloyd Loom style, white, covered in women's' worn clothes, underwear, headscarves and some sour towels. Far downstage left.

A four-foot wide vertical hanging of white gauze, suggestive of a French window, but also to be used as a backdrop to both the Trans-Lux and 'rape' sequences, just off the centre of the stage, upstage left.

Prominent piles of displaced things: books/record albums/photos/handbags/framed pictures – not too much, but all chaotic and without structure or design. Department store shopping bags (plain is fine, but Bloomingdales or Jax if you can find/make them) being used as storage: full of clothes, shoes, make-up, personal effects.

ESSENTIAL, PRACTICAL ITEMS

A white early 1960s US style telephone on the bed. Practical.
A period bedside lamp. Practical.
A 1950s/1960s compact mirror on the bed.
A glass of water by the bedside table.
A glass of water by the chair.
Practical pill bottles by the bedside table, by the chair and in the pocket of Marilyn's dressing gown.
Sticks of gum in the pocket of Noodle's dressing gown.
Large, used ashtray by bedside table.
Cigarette case with cigarettes.

OTHER ITEMS

Books to include: *To Kill a Mockingbird* by Harper Lee (which she is currently reading). If you want to be really flash – and can get hold of pre-August 1962 editions – then have books by any of the following: Shelley, Whitman, Keats, Thomas Wolfe, James Joyce, Dostoyevsky, Salinger, GB Shaw. *How Stanislavsky Directs* by Michael Gorchakov. Plays by Arthur Miller, Tennessee Williams. Art books on: Picasso, El Greco, Michelangelo, Botticelli. Some books she owned at time of death: Flaubert's *Madame Bovary;* Conrad's *The Secret Agent;* Beckett's *The Unnameable;* Flender's *Paris Blues;* Anderson's *Winesburg, Ohio;* Dreiser's *Sister Carrie;* Hemingway's *A Farewell to Arms* and *The Sun Also Rises;* Steinbeck's *Tortilla Flat* and

Once There Was A War; Camus' *The Fall;* Ellison's *Invisible Man;* Kerouac's *On the Road.*

Photo representing Joe DiMaggio's son / Photo representing Arthur Miller's son and daughter (These were found in this room after her death).

Large, very visible picture of Abraham Lincoln.

Amongst the record albums: Frank Sinatra, Judy Garland, Ella Fitzgerald, Mel Torme, Louis Armstrong, Earl Bostick. Less copiously, Mozart, Ravel, Bartok, Beethoven's symphonies. Note that Marilyn disliked 'modern' stuff like The Everly Brothers and Elvis, so avoid. (Incidentally, her favourite songs are known to include: Who Cares *by Judy Garland and* That's Why the Lady Is a Tramp *by Sinatra).*

A very bright A5 size red diary, discarded, but noticeable to the audience, if not Noodle.

Shoes and a pair of weathered fluffy slippers (not necessarily next to each other).

Clothes (if you can really go for it, then she would have had pale-green slacks – from Jax – and a cashmere sweater). Her favourite colours: white, black, orange, beige, red.

Make-up and cosmetics – especially Nivea face cream.

Chanel No 5 and/or Arpege bottle/s – these will be sprayed around the set before each performance and be worn by the performer, to allow the audience to smell her.

AVOID

Pictures of the real Marilyn – they will always *conflict with and undermine the authority of the performer. (You might want to bear this in mind when it comes to publicity too – any production's aims should include replacing the real Marilyn in the minds of the audience with our Noodle; basically I'm saying don't use her in your posters).*

Champagne bottles/glasses – no booze consumed this night and we don't want to suggest even the possibility.

Any of the clothing she wore in her movies – unless used creatively, i.e. separate from the performer's actual 'reality'.

LIGHTING

Natural light from 'outside' (8pm, California) that gradually gets darker, descending into total gloom by the end of the play. The second half is additionally lit by a practical table lamp, but 'outside', it continues to get darker.

NOODLE

Thirty-six-years-old, about 5ft 5½ inches tall. Blue/blue-grey eyes. Bleached blonde hair – champagne silver – cut into a long-ish bob, dry, messy, like candyfloss. Undeniably attractive, but nothing like her screen persona – or even carefully created interview/off-screen persona. This is Noodle, the unkempt, scruffy girl-woman who lives as she pleases in her own home and owes nothing to nobody. Not here to captivate, titillate or delight. Here to stomp about her own bedroom with no one taking pictures of her or gossiping about her.

She is, within the context of the play, wearing no make-up. If stage make-up helps solidify the performer within this role, then fair enough, but this play is built upon the strict paradigm that this is NOT the Marilyn everyone expects; this is Noodle. Stage make-up may be used to sharpen the performer's own eyes mouth and lips and bone structure, but it mustn't look like the character is made up. Far from it. In fact...

It is worth noting – and, if possible, attempting to achieve a look based upon these notes – that Marilyn had relatively thick, downy hair running down the side of her ears (sideburns, if you will), bleached to help disguise it. Also very freckly on face, neck, chest and arms, but not actually tanned. Legs much shorter than you'd expect. Toenails and fingernails painted.

It is important that she has blotchy skin on cheekbones – an aggravated skin condition that affects her in new situations (of which this is one). We're not talking Singing Detective, *but ruddiness needs to be apparent. MUSTN'T appear as if it is blusher. It should be there, but not draw attention to itself until Noodle points it out.*

Wearing old white towelling bathrobe (belt and pockets). It is grubby, stained with food and cosmetics. Practical pill bottles stuffed in the pockets. Underneath the robe, she would wear nothing, but for the sake of the performer's modesty, a white bra and pants is fine, but must be appropriate to 1962.

She will drink only water during the play – no booze. Marilyn, unusually, drank no booze on the night of her death.

Her voice is categorically NOT the breathy baby voice from her movies, or the tentative voice sometimes used in interviews. It's a relaxed Hollywood, California accent, tinged with a little New York picked up from her years on the East Coast. Any voices she imitates during the play will be accurate or at least plausible, relative to her grogginess. They must sound like the work of a brilliant observer and mimic. They must betray the acting abilities of a criminally underused talent.

She also suffers with a nervous stammer. As this play is not about her stammer, but the stammer is central to the character, the script denotes moments when Noodle struggles to find words in the stage directions. Please do not add any more. Note also that she will tail off her sentences or repeat words. These are all coping strategies she uses to avoid the stammer.

NB: Where the text states '(thinks)', this is essentially a meter for the speed at which the play is read on the page and denotes a change of introspective direction or a sudden moment of clarity. These instructions can be regarded/disregarded at the director's discretion.

When we meet her, she is pretty much as normal; alert and in the moment, if a little groggy at first (having just awoken). She brightens up as things get going – by which point she is as charming and radiant and full of life as we might expect her to be, if occasionally melancholy. She is bright and intelligent and energetic. She is neither stupid, crazy, irrational or... Sexy? Well, in the natural way that most people have the ability to be, but sex is what she does, not what she is. She's more likely to strike a pose that lampoons sex, undermines it, makes it grotesque than she is to actually put 'sexy' on. We're not going for Sex Goddess here, but aiming for a regular girl – with the charm, wit and energy of (and here's the buzz phrase) a natural clown. She has to be sympathetic and likeable. As welcoming, casual and charismatic as possible, regardless of what she is saying. Accessible. Disarming. Vulnerable. We should want to be in her company, even when she's annoyed or angry. Mostly, she's optimistic about the past – except where it really hurt – but she doesn't bear grudges. She's in the process of moving on and hopes for the best. Yes, she's very worried about her current career, but she is categorically NOT suicidal. Laughter rules her spirit, and she laughs and giggles a lot, especially when she's pleased with herself.

But even though we're trying to pull as far back from the icon as we can get, we're not trying to uglify or make her look foolish. She's a normal, regular woman, free to be herself and happy to be so.

Lesson over. On with the show…

NOODLE *(Marilyn), lying face down on the bed and partially turned away from us, in a stained white dressing gown, already looks dead.*

She's not. She's been taking pills and she's passed out.

There's a white telephone by her left hip. Her left hand holds the telephone receiver by her left ear, her right arm holds an open compact mirror. Her legs are 'crossed' behind her.

As the lights come up – just enough time for audience to notice that receiver and cradle are not connected – the telephone, inexplicably, rings. One ring, another ring. She makes groggy, responsive noises; an arm lurches into life. We don't see her face immediately; we only recognise the idea of her. Some business as she feels for the phone, realises she had it in her hand already and then pulls the receiver to her left ear (never realising that it shouldn't have rung). She answers after the fourth ring.

Bobby? Hello? Four-Seven-Six-One-Eight-Nine-Oh, hello? *(beat)* Speak up, I can't –

She listens for a moment.

(loud, over the static) Who is this? Pete?

She finally hears the voice at the other end: a static-heavy distortion of her own voice singing I Wanna Be Loved by You *(the audience can barely hear it let alone discern what it is). She scrambles up from lying down (her back to the audience).*

All right, you've had your fun.

She listens a moment longer, and then, turning, slams the phone into its cradle.

(softly) Goodbye.

She perches on the stage right edge of the bed still holding the phone, not quite looking out front (because she won't notice the audience for a few more moments).

1

A moment's thought. She picks up the receiver and begins to dial. A few digits in, she looks up and notices (something in the direction of) the audience. This takes her not exactly by surprise, but she now realises she is being watched.

Oh.

She stops dialling and slowly replaces the receiver, leaves telephone on bed.

She steps downstage, towards the audience, trying to focus through the 'wall' in front of her.

Now that's really…

Closes one eye, opens it; closes the other, opens it.

That *is* weird.

Steps back, only slightly nervous, but cautious nonetheless.

As the play commences, she'll adjust her dressing gown modestly, pay some vague lip service to a notion of presentability, and emerge from her grogginess to be caught up in the actions and physicalities of her stories and memories.

I can see you. Has this happened before?

She turns to look at the bed, then back at the audience.

Was I asleep just now? *(thinks)* Be a miracle if I was, because… *(beat)* Am I making *any* sense? I must've… passed out… *(looks back at bed)* Which is a good thing… I guess. At least something still works. *(thinks)* I should call Pete. We were talking and I…

Looks across at clock on bedside table.

(fidgety) Maybe I should go down to the beach. There's still time. *(thinks)* Maybe not. *(to herself)* Hold tight, Noodle.

(to audience) Was I making noises? I sleep with my mouth open. Were there noises? I'm pretty sure I was dreaming… *(looks hard at the bed)* No. Gone. *(gestures at phone)* Can you believe that? I was hoping it might be Bobby. I've been hoping all day. I just want to hear the smile in his voice. Y'know? But I guess you know how things've been…

When he last came to Pete's, I was so excited, but he seemed…
cautious. Around me, I mean. He didn't laugh or get silly…
It was over, not that he said so, but… I think someone had
something on him. Y'know? And being seen with me wasn't
doing him any favours. *(with amused irony)* So I'm a whore
now. Because that's what we call single women who enjoy the
company of married men. I mean, c'mon! In 1962? Is that the
best we can do? The best *he* can do? Ignore my calls? Rather
than stand up and say, 'She's my friend, folks. We laugh, we
get silly. That is *all*.' I'm so mad at Bobby. His brother, too.
Courageous and brilliant, but cowards over women. Like we're
only convenient with the lights out. Right? If the spotlight
catches us both in the same glare, then it's bye-bye, baby. And
then they're scared you'll spill their secrets, like they have
any worth spilling. And that's so typical of some guys. It's all
about them. *(thinks)* Maybe we should love them less. Not that
it's physical. Yes, he's handsome, but… Well, he's too skinny.
I didn't go after him like I went after Yves. We just kind of
washed up together.

Pete invited me to one of his beach parties. Like tonight, but
a campaign thing… he'd just married Pat. A great night, but
I get pretty nervous around all these… minds. Y'know? I was
knocked out when Pat said 'Meet my brother'. I mean… Jack
Kennedy! What a guy! But we talked… And I liked him. He
liked me, too, but it was never deep. His teeth are too perfect.
I don't know. Y'know?

But the press grab what they can… eyes full of dollar signs –
ker-ching! – like cartoons. They want it to be an affair, because
that sells papers and makes them powerful, so whether or not
we are, it's official: JFK's doing the Noodle. And because I won't
answer the questions they want answered, they feel vindicated
in their assertions. They don't think for a second that I'm just
a friend – a good friend, yes – and that I'd like to honour that
friendship by zipping my lips and making sure I don't get in
the way of his ambitions. No, I'm looking for a bedroom in the
White House, and meek acquiescence from his beautiful wife.
His *perfect* wife. Result? Noodle loses a friend because now she's
a liability. And that's how I ended up with Bobby.

*Smiling, she takes a stick of gum from her dressing gown pocket, sits on
the end of the bed, and chews as she talks.*

He was awkward and shy. He doesn't come across that way on television, but he's so sweet and nervous. His background's more privileged than mine, but I respect what he's doing for this country. *He's* the genius. Jack gets the attention, but it's Bobby that makes things happen.

His sister laughed when the press said we were lovers, but how irresponsible is that? Of the press, I mean. Bobby's wife didn't deserve that. After that, if we needed to talk, it was telephones all the way. We'd talk for hours some days. A sympathetic ear. Maybe part of me was looking for a scandal. Y'know? Maybe that's why I can see you right now. I mean, it was scandal that brought you here in the first place. Trouble is, keeping you around requires a steady supply. I'm thirty-six. Younger guys still whistle, but scandal and sensation don't come easy. But that's no bad thing. Right?

Animatedly, she gets up off the bed and comes downstage.

D'you mind me talking like this? It's good to get things out there. I don't sleep well. Even with pills, and I shouldn't be taking *them*. I should take something to wake me up. But then I'd have to take something to stop me buzzing and I'd only lie awake all night. *(thinks)* What did I take this afternoon?

She looks over the selection of pills on or by the bedside table, getting rid of her gum in an ashtray.

More than I need, that's for sure. Ralph's prescription, my internist's prescription... *(thinks)* Maybe just a smoke. *(sits on the bed by the table, distractedly removing a small pill bottle from her pocket)* I've been a little down, I'll admit. Drifting. I hate living alone. I kept the New York apartment, just in case, but it was time to... come back, I guess. *(she has removed a pill and now takes it, swallowing it dry)* I was missing the ocean. The sound it makes... like home... like me. The me I remember being. Now, I've got eight rooms, a pool, a wall to hide behind and an anonymous mailbox. Okay, so really it belongs to the bank, but the mortgage is mine. And the renovation costs. So, sorry about the mess. *(gestures theatrically at the chaos of her room)* Thing is, you get used to it. Mostly, it's just me and Maf. Dogs beat husbands, that's for sure. No dog ever told me to shut up, let me tell you. Except Eunice. She can be a bitch.

Silences herself; she's spoken out of turn too loudly. Quickly tip-toes upstage right to 'door' and listens. Waves hand dismissively and quickly returns downstage to audience, acting like a child going behind its parent's back.

(quieter, at first) My housekeeper. She's been spying on me. I told Ralph – my head doctor? – but he won't hear it. Eunice was his idea. She drives me out there for treatment. *(thinks)* I guess she could be spying on me for *him*, but he *knows* all my secrets. *(thinks)* Maybe not.

(highly animated again) Maybe I should go to the beach? Drinks, good music, running gags... Everyone'll be there. And I like to be with people. Trouble is, the only people I ever got *really* close to were my husbands. Or other women's husbands. Or men who wanted to *be* my husband. There's never been anyone I could share *everything* with. *(looks directly at an audience member)* You, maybe, but sometimes I wish *you'd* go away. Imagine that relief. Not having to constantly start over. Hah! Right now, all I do is wish I was back at Fox six days a week. *(sad)* This sitting around and waiting is like starving outside Romanoff's with the smell of good spaghetti driving me crazy. *(thinks)* Like I need spaghetti for that...

(brighter) I'm hoping to be in Huston's Freud movie. Sartre's writing the script, can you believe that? He thinks I'm great, if no one else does. Ralph says, "Don't do it, Freud wouldn't approve", but he's reading too much into it. Sometimes a movie's just a movie. But if I don't, there's plenty to keep me busy. Hey, I even posed nude for *Vogue*! What can I say? Ten years ago it would've ruined my career, now I'm hoping it'll save it. Not that I'm good at being naked these days.

She sits on the end of the bed and takes the pill bottle from her pocket.

In my last picture there's this pool scene. Fox thinks it'll be more 'realistic' if I swim nude, no flesh suit. I should say no, but they're in trouble because Liz Taylor's causing a stink on *Cleopatra*. The only thing between them and bankruptcy is my bare tush. *(she has removed a pill and takes it, dry, whilst talking)* But I'm on a hundred thou' a crummy picture, while the chick making trouble banks an epic million. I'm supposed to swallow this? They'll make a fortune on my name alone, but still they want me to skinny dip. And d'you know what? I swallow. I strip and do my duty. Like old times...

I don't suppose you saw, but I was terrified. They expect so much, because of the image... bells and whistles... but I'm the same as any woman. Being exposed like that... What if I got so anxious I... *(searches for words, which makes her almost stammer, so she changes tack)* If, y'know... my guts played up? Scratch one Sex Goddess. So, every morning, nerves... throwing up at the gate. I say my throat's bad, to get time off... think things through. But then they're back to telling me I'm difficult. I wish someone had taken me aside – just... just once in all these years – and said 'Hey, what's wrong?' I could've told them. Not that a goddess should talk about that stuff...

So, because all their eggs are in one basket, the studio's patience wears thin. It's non-existent when I skip school to sing 'Happy Birthday' at Madison Square Garden. But what's more important? A day's filming or the President's birthday?

The following Monday, I can't go in. My belly's in turmoil, but I also have a temperature and... *(gets up from bed, moving downstage, furiously)* Fox blows its stack. No one believes me, so they send a doctor who says I have a virus. Three days later, I've been fired for 'wilful violation' and they're lying about me in the press. I 'don't care' about the people whose jobs depend on me... I'm 'deliberately' trying to ruin them – like I can control that! Do they mention *Cleopatra?* No. If you get sick, you get sick. It's not easy moving from picture to picture, working Hollywood hours. It's okay when *They* get sick. But when Noodle gets sick... *(struggles to find the words, can't)* The gossips lap it up. It's everything they've hoped for.

Wearily, she goes and sits in the chair.

It was the same when Clark died. The press blamed *me.* Like I pushed a pillow to his face. I'd been 'difficult' on *Misfits* and that caused the heart attack – even though we'd been wrapped a month. *(she takes a pill, dry, from a bottle next to the chair)* No one called Monty 'difficult', or Huston. Better if it's 'the troubled Ms. Monroe'. A rehash of everything I went through with Johnny. I ask you: what mechanisms are in place that allow a person to respond to this... horrible stuff? I'll tell you: there are none. Not one.

Clark was my friend. He stood by me when I was anxious. And you would be anxious, wouldn't you? If you were me? On set, with your dead marriage dangling in your face? A director who's *(as John Huston:)* 'Honey, this', 'Honey, that', treating you like an idiot and arguing with your coach, while your husband flirts with a photographer, and it's boiling hot, and Monty Clift's dying in front of you. I was messed up, sure, but he was in bits and that's not right, is it? Not if you're as beautiful and talented as Monty. *(thinks)* Poor Monty. I don't know where things will go for him. He has a lot of problems and a lot of addictions that don't help those problems. And that's kinda scary. A toss of the dice and we fall apart. But Clark was there if I blew a line. And when I was late. Yeah, shoot me, quick, before the world ends. I don't choose to be late. Stuff happens and... *(struggles with words, desperately trying not to stammer)* I shouldn't be in pictures if it's going to churn me up like that. It's the opposite of glamorous.

So they're calling me arrogant for missing work... I'm all blasé... blaming Norma Jeane for taking a bubble bath or something. *(sudden flashing anger)* I was in hospital... you idiots! The solutions to *my* problems brought problems of their own. I was... *(stammering now, painfully and shockingly caught up in her own inability to get the words out properly)* I felt so... disappointed. In myself. I felt a duty... to Clark, of all people. Like I was... keeping my... father waiting. Right? *(stammering ends)* I guess I could've turned up... but no one would've got their money's worth. Not from that woman. That woman was no sex symbol. She symbolised nothing. And if I'm on set, I'm there to work and work hard, but that poor girl... she had nothing to give.

Misfits was their movie, you see, their great work. Arturo's and Huston's. The most expensive black and white ever made. On paper, it was cowboys killing horses for dog food. They didn't need me. Not physically. They just needed two magic words to sell it: 'Marilyn Monroe'. And I've never forgiven Arthur for writing me another pathetic blonde. Unintelligent, thrashing, crying... That's the best he could do for me? And the women watching? I expect a little more from my progressive thinkers. *(thinks)* I guess there was more emotion than usual. But Huston still had the camera on my tush.

That shoot was full of so-called men, but only one of them ever brought me a chair. Clark. He was a hero worth the name. Arthur wasn't. Not anymore. *(gets out of the chair and goes downstage centre)* When we wrapped the picture, we wrapped the marriage. No fuss. But when Clark died, I crumpled like a grocery bag. Three marriages down, no one to turn to, no one to hold, no one to put me at the centre of things, and the press accusing me of murder. *(pause)* So I took an overdose and killed myself.

Telephone rings. Excitedly she scampers to pick it up, on the stage left side of the bed.

Four-Seven-Six-One-Eight-Nine-Oh.

We hear the very vague, distorted, crackly song being played at her, but can't identify it. She's disturbed, but annoyed.

(trying to communicate across the static) Who is this? Where... How did you get this number? Hello?

Slams receiver down. Holds it there. Pause. Lifts receiver, listens. Nothing. Replaces it. Thinks, then, with a flash of excited happiness, remembers she was talking to audience.

(light and breezy) Ten Seconal pills, ten Tuinal pills. A clean death. No cutting, I'm too vain. If I hadn't survived... The overdose, I mean... Would the press have blamed themselves for my death? Would anyone have accused *them* of *my* murder? No. They'd have built theories and made up stories and a million and one people would've staked a claim on the drama that left me dead. *(thinks)* The woman who took those pills was another person, but those memories sting. Somewhere underneath all this, she still hurts.

(thrilled at being able to act this out, which she does) They sent me to Payne-Whitney. If I'd known it was a head hospital, I'd have run a mile... So I walk in, giving them the full Marilyn and they're all smiles and cups of tea and 'Just sign here please'. Before I know it, I'm in a padded cell – on the dangerous floor with the girl who slits her throat. My clothes and purse are gone. I'm thrown in a bath, manhandled and left in a gown with my derriere on show. And they're watching through the window like I'm a nut. Like I'm Jimmy Stewart in *Harvey*. I'm sick and they know best. It took everything I had to place the call that got me out.

You know Arthur's married again? *(she sits on the end of the bed)* To that photographer I caught him with. She's pregnant. Well, good luck to them. *(taking a pill from the bottle in a pocket, she 'toasts' them and swallows it)* Good luck to *her. (thinks)* Maybe she needs less than I do. Now I sound like a bitch. *(thinks)* It wasn't his fault. Or hers. It was over before *Misfits.* Gossips circling the perimeter as usual. He took me to see Yves Montand on Broadway, and they wrote that I was 'smitten'. They were right, I was. With Yves, I mean. That honey-dripping accent... Wow! I saw that show a couple of times, and those tickets cost a buck or two, believe me. He just seemed so... delicious. Like Arthur, but draped in chocolate and dipped in jimmies. And French, obviously. Arthur knew Yves and Simone so getting them to dinner wasn't hard. We got along swell, but... Well, you know how I felt about Yves. Goose pimply all over. All he had to do was touch my arm or... Gee, the guy only had to stare into space and I was his. So I suggested him for *Let's Make Love.* It was the only way to get him to myself. Arthur was in Ireland, and Simone was in Europe. What can I say? I fell in love.

It must've hurt Arthur... to read about his Poopsie being romanced by another guy. But this is Hollywood. 'You can't make a movie without breaking hearts'. The night before we wrapped, Yves made love to me. *(as Yves Montand:)* 'You're everything I want, everything I've ever dreamed of.' Next day, he's moved out and gone back to Paris – to Simone. Do you know what that... what that feels like? I'd been charmed, seduced... and discarded like some... spent emotion in a scrunched up tissue. I was business as usual to him – and Simone... another acquisition in a run of acquisitions. And I hate him for that. Even now. Not that I've heard from him since. *(pause)* But if he walked in here, arms open... I'd... I'd fall right in all over again. Beautiful, sexy, adorable... bastard. *(pause, before smiling)* Oh, it made an awful picture bearable. Mr Cukor – the director – he didn't like me. He'd been got at. I never gave him reason... He just doesn't *want* to like me. Directors get like that. But Cukor's not the worst. That honour goes to Mr Wilder.

(gets off bed and hurries downstage, excited to be able to share) Okay, I've never told anyone this, but when Wilder asked me to do *Some Like It Hot* I was in two minds. All I could see was a blonde so dumb she mistook Tony Curtis for a chick. I mean, there's

dee-you-em-bee and there's Dumb. And what kind of idiot did I want to look like? Arthur said it would stop me moping. And, gee, we needed the money. Writers don't bring much in. *(thinks)* They bring *nothing* in.

Wilder said I was hell to work with, and I'm sure I was, with… Well, one thing and another. Acting anxieties, the physical stuff… It hurt so much I couldn't stand straight. But Wilder wouldn't let me forget that I was keeping everyone waiting. If they'd… known… what I was going through… They treated me like I didn't know I was an inconvenience. I'd've given anything to change that. But some of the people on that movie were just plain cruel.

Like Tony. Wilder turned him, too. *(in Tony Curtis's Cary Grant accent)* 'Kissing Marilyn is like kissing Hitler'? Can you believe that? *(to an audience member)* Maybe you can. But what does it mean? I have a moustache? Bad hair? I have both, but was kissing *him* any better? Love scenes are easy if there's an attraction. You like each other, you laugh together… If not, the trick is to imagine you're kissing someone else. I don't remember who I was kissing, but it sure wasn't Tony. *(thinks)* 'Hitler'!

And to throw salt in the sugar, I got pregnant again. Not exactly an over the moon moment. You lose one baby, you're only scared of losing the next. The last thing I needed was work… Or Wilder going public: *(as Billy Wilder, in his thick German accent:)* 'She's late for this, thirty takes for that'.

(laughing) At the premiere, the press could only fix on the fact that Art and I arrived late. Big joke. No one stopped to… *(darker now)* Well, I lost that baby too, right? The only thing we ever wanted – baby Miller – and twice it was snatched away. They never once considered that we might not want to be there, pretending life was swell. *(laughing as a way of compensating for the pain of the memories)* It was agony. And the operations… *(pause)* It was hell. A dark pit you couldn't climb out of because it was inside you. I needed my husband's love. But… Arthur was at the end of everything he had to give. Which meant I was, too. *(sits in chair)* I sat in the dark for a year.

(smiles) I was sitting in the dark when he first found me. *(she takes another dry pill from the bottle by the chair)* After Johnny died.

I was on a picture, but I couldn't stop crying. Art came on set with Elia Kazan. He was quiet… grand – like Lincoln. Y'know? But without the beard. I was a mess. He never forgot that. A couple of nights later, I saw him at a party. I couldn't believe how high my heart jumped. He was so… refreshing. Married, of course, but he didn't patronise me, not like the actors I knew. We sat on a sofa, all curled up. *(points her foot)* See this toe? He held it as he talked, not bold enough to rub the whole foot. We just sat and talked – ignored everyone else – all evening. I'd live through an entire marriage before Art got the whole foot.

She gets out of the chair and bouncily, giddily comes downstage.

Five years later, I was in New York. *Seven Year Itch* was huge, and I was making big money. For Fox, not me. I was the biggest thing they had. Still am if my tush is the solution to their woes. I wanted better money – not because I'm greedy – getting off a starlet's wages meant script approval, director choice… So I walked, and New York was where *real* acting happened.

So it's just after Christmas when Sam Spade walks me over Brooklyn Bridge. It may be raining – like, horizontal rain – but it's perfect. To get dry and maybe something hot to drink, we go see an old buddy of his. That's how I meet Claude – and Hedda. Sam doesn't tell them who I am, in case it throws them. He's a photographer, I'm his model. He mumbles, so they don't hear my name right. All afternoon they're calling me Marion. *(shrugs)* It's beautiful. They accept me for who I am… *(to the audience)* before *you* can get in the way. They've been my best friends ever since. I want them to see the house. If I knew they were coming I'd make it ready.

She goes to the bed, grabs a pillow to hug to herself, takes another stick of gum to chew, and sits on the end of the bed all chatty like she's at a sleepover with girlfriends.

So anyway, they have this fabulous soirée and introduce me to a friend of theirs. And it's Arthur. They don't know we've already met. He's still married, but he falls in love with me. It works both ways, y'know? It's not just about me being impressed because he's a thinker and he's amazing and… And his legs go on for ever and he makes me giggle till I hurt. It's about him glowing like a child when he's near me. That was the first time I fell in love. I mean *love*. *(thinks)*

Through Arthur, I met Lee at the Actors Studio. Back then, Lee was like… like a guru… a father. But he could kill you with a word. *(thinks)* He's so ambitious. I couldn't see that then. I adore him, I do, but… *(gets off bed, leaves pillow and comes downstage)* I was supposed to be in this television play he said he was directing. This summer. He said it was a done deal, but it wasn't. And there's me, re-arranging my life… *(thinks)* I don't know. If it wasn't for Lee I'd still be a dumb blonde. *(considers)* I *am* still a dumb blonde! But I was a good ambassador for his studio. Good publicity. And I worked hard.

Not that everyone took me seriously. *(a selection of outraged New York voices:)* 'She's *choosing* to improve herself?' 'She's scrubbed off the make-up?' 'She's in baggy clothes?' *(knowingly)* I guess they couldn't see past my definitive Monroe. *(thinks)* The other members avoided me, I don't know why. Maybe they were being polite. Or playing it cool, they excelled at that. And they never applauded. Members would play brilliant scenes and I'd want to cheer or clap or whistle, but there'd be this… silence, while everyone waited for Lee's reaction. Maybe they couldn't look me in the eye without his permission or something? Or it could have been the rash. Important occasion? Bam! My skin flares up. Stop press: the most beautiful woman in the world has scabby cheeks. Not looking good is it? People expect too much. Period pains, irritable bowels, insomnia, scabby skin… They tend to come as a shock. *(sudden moment of being watched, criticised)* It's there now, isn't it?

Self-consciously touching her face, she rushes to the stage right edge of the bed, picks up the compact and has a look at herself, whilst also getting rid of her gum in the ashtray.

Sheesh. I'm all out of Calamine. I *drank* the stuff at the Actors Studio.

She puts the compact back on the bed and comes back downstage, still unconsciously touching her cheeks for a few moments.

A few months in, Lee and I put together a piece from *Anna Christie*. A tough piece. Anna goes through stuff I went through… as a little girl. And… something deep… and difficult… twists in me, as I play it out to those cool, beautiful actors. When I reach the end, I know I've done *something* right because I *felt* that girl, I *was* her. But as Anna makes her way out of my… nervousness, I hear a new sound, unexpected… All those incredible people – clapping. At me. So loudly. Even the girls who came to confirm my… uselessness. Wiping tears from eyes that are usually frozen. The kind of actors that never praise you. That insecurity of being too generous about another actor's work. Like it might somehow devalue their own efforts. It's an odd thing, a theatre thing, but actors hold their cards to their chest. The joke's on them, though, because they all have the same cards. Card one: I. Card two: Am. Card three: The. Card four: Best. It's not arrogance… it's a cue card, a prompt, a goal. A need. We're so scared of losing the next job to someone less deserving… Which as far we're concerned is everyone, because to do this we have to believe we're the unassailable best. Or what's the point? So I'm standing in a room full of unassailable bests and they're hugging me, loving me, rewarding me. After that, Hollywood was just the office. New York was home.

(goes back to the bedside table) When Arthur suggested marriage, people said I was desperate to marry America. *(takes a pill from the bottle in her pocket, chasing it down with a swig of water from the glass by the bed)* Again. But who best symbolised America then? Miller or Monroe? *(sitting on the stage right edge of the bed, she takes a pill from a bottle on or by the bedside table, crunching it loudly)* I'm not saying he did it to look heroic, but I hate the way people assume it was about me trying to look intelligent. It was just one piece of the American jigsaw puzzle fitting another. Fox told me to keep away from him. They were scared because he'd been hauled up in court. Sure he had – for *thinking* the wrong way. Those bastards will always be cowards. I stood by Arthur through that whole sham. If I hadn't covered his costs, there would be no Arthur Miller.

Animated and chatty, she jumps up from the bed and comes downstage.

We got married twice. Once in New York and again in Connecticut where we did the Jewish part. Art's not religious, but *I* believe, so I converted. Soon as I did, they banned my films in Egypt. It was okay to look at the pretty lady until she married a Jew. Maybe kissing Egypt would be like kissing Hitler?

We honeymooned in London, because I was shooting my first movie there! For my own company, I mean. London airport exploded. People climbing over tables to get close. And that's just the press! The Brits were happy to see us, but, boy, were they happy when we left. You know what Larry's like... We deliberately chose him to play the lead. I'd see a movie starring Olivier and Monroe, right? We even got Larry to direct. Bad move.

And I was so scared. People think we go out there, and you know, just do it. But I struggle. And the insomnia's bad, so I'm late on set, and if it isn't that it's my period, or I've eaten something I shouldn't, or I'm just plain terrified that I'm as bad an actor as they think I am. I spend half my life locked in bathrooms, creased up in pain and blood and fear and who knows what else. And Larry's no director. He's afraid to say what he feels. To my... to my face. No, he *performs* his anxiety... puts me down to everyone else... refuses to be direct so I can have my say. Maybe *he* wants to be the pretty blonde in the tight white dress? She has the better part. The best she's had. Arthur's good though, I'll give him that. Larry doesn't respect me, but he respects Arthur. So Art steps in and makes things happen my way. *(thinks)* Heh. I say he's good... That time with the notebook kinda blows a hole in things. And he's a writer. It's not just what he does, it's what he *is*. He's making notes while we shoot... Character studies. And they're sharp, y'know? Precise. I shouldn't peek, but I do, and... I guess I'm looking for something wonderful from a love-struck husband for his new bride. But this is Mr Miller. It's difficult. Hard to swallow, y'know? Like he's disappointed in me. And he's been honest about everyone else, but I'm... I'm his wife. He's supposed to love me no matter what. Like I love him... no matter what.

She sits, thoughtfully, on the end of the bed and takes another pill, dry, from the bottle in her pocket.

He'd decided that the angel he'd married was... Well, not the angel he *thought* he'd married. Not that I *claimed* to be an angel. So... the only thing disappointing the earthy, intellectual genius was his own... unbridled... romanticism. Right? But it hurt, and it shouldn't have, because now I can see why he wrote that, but... *(thinks)* But what, Max? *(thinks)* He was wrong. He was wrong about me. And the reason I got upset was... was because the man I'd chosen to... live my life with, the man I'd stood by... under the worst kind of scrutiny... had failed to understand me. I got over it pretty quickly, but the moment I read those words... I had nowhere left to hide. If I lost a line or... If I said something unkind because I felt... let down or... got-at, then it was flung back at me. Twice as hard and in the press. *(gets up, angrily, and comes downstage)* It was okay to treat me like an imbecile, but if I expressed *my* opinions about the way things were running on *my* picture... *(suddenly, impossibly, bright and calm)* But, hey. Whatever they said, whatever they did, however ill they made me, that picture won awards. And the Showgirl acts the Prince right off the screen. You know it.

She slumps into the chair and drinks some water.

After that, Arthur and I took a year out. We spent a lot of time in East Hampton. With Hugo! I loved Hugo. He was always depressed, I don't know why. I mean, he had the biggest set of balls I ever saw. Huge. Maybe that was the problem. They hung so low, they'd drag on the concrete. I guess I'd be depressed if I was always catching my bits and pieces on stones and twigs. I was forever picking him up. The only thing that cheered him up was whiskey. Big balls, whiskey and a movie star making a fuss of him. He should've been happy, but I guess the thing that stopped that working for him was... Well he was a dog. *(sudden realisation; embarrassed but naughty)* Did I say he was my dog? Hugo was my dog. *(thinks)* I'd been stung by Art, but I loved him and it was still physical. I still had problems, you know. I'll spare your blushes, but... I could satisfy Arthur, but I still had trouble getting there myself. Right? *(with irony)* Sex Goddess. Not that I really *get* sex. I just need cuddles and nuzzles and kisses. Even when you're not making love, love can still be made.

(suddenly downbeat) You know how far I fell when the pain came. When I lost the first baby. *(thinks)* Whole days in the park, watching children play. *(pause)* When the doctor said we could give it another shot, I wanted to scream. Like trying again would make things okay. I think Arthur blamed me, I don't know.

(gets out of chair and comes downstage) Call me old-fashioned – and I can be – but a husband and wife should share the same bed. We even stopped eating together. It was like his love had died and he'd replaced me with silence. If Hedda held a party, I'd get him along, but he wouldn't dance. Not that he liked dancing, but a drink would help him find the mood. That scene in *Bambi*, where he's all tangled up on the ice? A dozen more legs and that was Arthur. But now I was dancing with strangers, when all I wanted was everyone to see me dance with him. He wouldn't even touch me. It was Joe all over again.

The sudden shift of topic makes her miraculously upbeat and energised. And as she continues, she sits on the end of the bed and takes another dry pill from the bottle in her pocket.

Hey, d'you know, it's ten years since I met Joe? I was only talking about this the other day, how I wasn't interested at first. My agent arranged dinner. Joe saw me posing with other ball players and wanted to know why he never got shoots like that. Come the night, I'm bushed and trying to get out of it, but I'd promised, so… *(self-aware)* Yeah, I was late. I get all ready for something and people tell me I look great, but I don't feel great and end up taking it off and starting all over again. Don't get me wrong, I *can* be late just for kicks. Not on set, but in other parts of my life. Especially if someone's eager to see me. It wasn't always like that, see? There were times when no one gave a damn about seeing me. And those times'll come again. I know that. So it's a miracle I got to Joe at all. I was expecting some loudmouth with slick hair… But he was a gentleman. Well-dressed. Tanned, but grey. Grey suit, grey tie, grey in his hair. His suit was broad in the shoulder to make him look bigger than he was. *(thinks)* Does he still do that? *(thinks)* But there was no angle, no jokes even. He was so serious. Like Arthur, he's not what you'd call handsome… with that goofy grin… but he was warm. Impeccable manners. I didn't have the first clue about baseball.

(as Joe:) 'That's okay, kid. I know even less about movies'. But then Mickey Rooney's gang spots us. They're all over Joe, fussing and reliving all these DiMaggio moments that meant so much to them. And you know Joe. When Mickey's gone, he's chasing exorbitant spaghetti around his plate like nothing happened, but I begin to understand just who I'm eating with.

And I'm not tired any more. I talk about Cary Grant and Joe talks about his restaurant. We laugh. We're having fun. We have dinner the next night, and the next night, and every night till he heads back East. And that's how Max and Joe got started. Thank God for Joe.

(gets up off the bed and comes downstage) I could see he didn't like the Marilyn part of me... the way they dressed me... or anything to do with Hollywood. When he mentioned marriage, I kinda stalled. My career was suddenly big business. *Photoplay* had just voted me Most Promising New Star. After seven years in pictures! So I'm at the dinner in this gold sheath dress, low cut. I'm a million dollars, but Joan Crawford's telling anyone who'll listen that I'm a disgrace. *(as Joan Crawford:)* 'She flaunts those tits like a hooker.' She misses out the part where, a few days before, she drops by and in the middle of a very polite cup of coffee, she grabs one of those offending boobs and gives it a squeeze. She shows me her stocking tops, I show her the door. So now she's complaining about my God-given attributes and Joe... Joe thinks she has a point! But that's who I was: the Marilyn that Fox built. Being *that* woman in *that* dress with *those* 'tits' was my *job*. For what it's worth – and I figured it was worth a hell of a lot – my box office was top five. Cooper, Crosby, Gardner, Hayward, Noodle. I was bigger than John Wayne, but I think Joe hoped I'd give it all up to be Finny the full time wife.

Soon as he had me on paper, that was it. Dating was a fairy tale – but the reality... of living together... Joe was... Well, he liked to stay home and watch sports. If he went out, it was all night poker. And if I liked a thing, it would annoy Joe. Reading! I wanted Joe to read, too, so we could talk... about Jules Verne or... Mickey Spillane, but he just wanted to watch the game...

(goes to chair, sits down and picks up pill bottle) I was hoping for love, I guess. Aren't we all? But Joe froze up. Like his heart was looking the other way. He wanted me to be like the girls he grew up with. He loved Noodle, but he didn't love Max. *(without water, she takes the pill she's removed from the bottle by the chair)* It's no secret that I can be untidy *(gestures at her messy room)* and he climbed on the back of that. Then his ulcer came back and he'd go days without a word, which is pretty weird, let me tell you. He spent more time with the television than he did with me, but that's regular for some guys, I guess. Till they move

into a different part of the house. Starting work on my next movie was like parole. But Joe missed me, and then he'd get bored and that made him grumpy. *(as Joe:)* 'I need a real wife, and you need a real job, so what's it gonna be? Me or those dumb movies?' *(pause)* That's all you need after a twelve hour day. But he got to me. If I was risking my marriage to stay in pictures, then they ought to be good pictures. I was desperate to do something that involved real clothes and walking straight.

(gets up from chair and stands centre stage) So he's calling me on set, shouting, like a little boy, and this is where *that* begins. Right? My guts churn up and I lose a day in the bathroom. Filming runs over, Fox get annoyed… But, hey, the picture makes more money than they put in and I move onto *Seven Year Itch*. Not that Joe's impressed. Rumbling and grumbling about the place like a television spot for Pepto-Bismol. *(thinks)* In the end, it was a skirt that pushed us apart.

She acts out the following, upstage left against the vertical white hanging. The ambient light has darkened and she is now lit by a spot.

So it's late one warm September night outside the Trans-Lux Theatre. The street should be quiet, but we've told the press what we're doing. Money can't buy that kind of attention. I'm standing in front of a thin line of police tape, behind which, four thousand New Yorkers pray for a glimpse of my panties. And as I wave at the crowd, I realise one of them is Joe. He smiles at me and I smile back. Then the fan sends air up through the subway grating and my big white skirt lifts and dances about my neck. Four thousand voices express wild delight and I realise this is something *big*. I'm exhilarated and excited. Nervous, oh sure, but caught up in the madness of the moment. It's a roller-coaster. I'm thrilled, but kinda happy when it's over. *(pause)* Then Mr Wilder insists on taking the shot again. And again and again. Four thousand voices get a little rowdier each time the camera closes in on my vagina. Luckily I'm wearing two pairs of white pants. My usual reasons, of course, but I'm also worried that my hair might poke out the sides. *(briefly coming out of the story she's setting up)* Not that I've seen the footage. They never used it. *(getting back into her story)* Anyway, the air drifts up and with it the skirt, over and over again, for longer than I'd like. The camera's moving out and then closing in on the sexiest part of the sex symbol. *(knowingly)* Out and in, out and in. And I'm pressing down on the fan-like, billowing folds of my skirt, protecting as much of my modesty as I can. Some guys – quite close to Joe – start calling out. Saying stuff, y'know? Remarks. Things you don't say to a person, and never in front of her husband. And they're whistling. Well, the best I can do is smile, laugh it off, but I'm not comfortable. I'm naked. So I look over to Joe, hoping to catch his eye and get some reassurance. And to reassure him back, because I know how he must be feeling. But when my eyes finally find him, he's turning his back on me. He's walking away. In disgust, I can tell. And now he's just one of the four thousand. And I'm alone. Alone amongst the yelps and yowls, all of them screaming my name. Alone in front of eight thousand eyes – and all of them focussed on my most private self. And I know, in that lonely moment, that my marriage must end.

The spot fades and the ambient light continues as before.

(she sits, forlorn, on the end of the bed) That night I slept alone. *(suddenly recalling)* And dreamt I was dead. Dressed in white... an open casket. And I knew, even without a mirror that I looked beautiful. That, in itself, was stranger than knowing I was dead, and that, damn, I wanted to be dead. Joe was there, but he was crying, and Joe *never* cries. He kissed me for the last time and told me he loved me... sobbing as I lay there, unable to do a single thing to help him. And he kept on telling me he loved me. Over and over.

(getting up, upbeat) Next morning, that skirt made front pages across the world. Sex was the new fun. Good, clean, American fun. Like soda pop and bubble bath. Like baseball.

It's dark now, so she goes and clicks on the bedside lamp. She then sits on that stage right side of the bed, taking a pill from the bottle in her pocket and sipping it with water.

When we separated, he'd ask people if I was seeing anyone. He couldn't accept that I'd ended it without there being someone else. In the end, he let me go and didn't contest. I've heard he still loves me. He hasn't told me himself, but... When I was locked up in Payne-Whitney, he was in Florida – coaching the

Yankees – but he flew straight back to New York and got me out. Thank God for Joe.

(sudden energy lifts her from the bed and brings her downstage) Losing him felt like a deal with the devil, because once he'd gone, my dream of stardom came true. Wilder threw me a party at Romanoff's. I'd finally arrived, see? And the whole aristocracy came: Gary Cooper, Bogie and Lauren… When they put Clark on my table, I came over like a teenager and asked for his autograph. Only if he could have mine! And I danced with him. *(thinks)* Gee, I even danced with Groucho.

You know about Groucho, right? When I was starting out, RKO needed a blonde for a Marx Brothers picture, so I talked Groucho into seeing me. There were three girls on the list and Groucho had us each walk away from him. We had to wiggle across a room. *(she demonstrates this as she talks)* I practised for a week. Groucho loved it so much he had me do it twice. He said I had the prettiest ass in the business, and I went along with that, but the guy had about a million hands. Everywhere I turn he's there. Groping and clinging. Being a finger buffet for older men gets creepy real quick, y'know? But I got the part. He even wrote me a line!

When Johnny Hyde saw that movie, he took me on straight away. Johnny was wonderful. Sophisticated, dapper… Intelligent… A true great. But he was so short that I'd wear flats so at least he'd come up to my chest when we danced. When no one was looking I'd sneak kisses onto his bald spot. He was so kind. *(she sits in the chair)* And that's maybe the hardest thing to find in life, kindness. Johnny knew all the dark… messy stuff inside me and loved me in spite of it. *(she takes a dry pill from the bottle by the chair somewhere here)* When… when he told me he loved me, I knew he meant it. But I didn't know what to do… I loved being with him, dancing, eating out… But I didn't want to be Mrs Hyde. Y'know? That post was filled. And the incumbent was citing me as 'the other woman'. But it'd been over for a long time. He begged me to marry him. *(as Johnny:)* 'I only have a few years. You'll inherit a fortune.' But how would that be fair? I cared for him and… Well, we had… moments, we did, but… If you're gonna marry, then do it because you love a person. Because you love yourself. Do it for love.

Animated and energetic again, she gets up from the chair, and starts acting stuff out.

Anyway, Johnny heard about *Asphalt Jungle*. Huston was directing and Johnny knew him so we went to see him. In those days, Huston sort of loomed over you like Karloff. Dark eyes, mussed up hair... Like he'd spent all morning in a bar. But he was a genius. My first. I was sick with nerves, but he said I looked right and offered me an audition. The part was all tears and breakdowns. Actors love that stuff. Natasha – my coach – and I decided I'd perform as if reclining on a couch.

So I walk into Huston's office – and there's no couch. My throat's tight. What would Natasha do? Think, Max, think. So I do it on the floor... and it's awful. Huston pushes me to the door, saying he'll be in touch, but I'm not hearing what he's saying. I'm pulling myself apart and just as he's closing me out, I march back in and ask to do it again. He says it won't be necessary. I tell him it will. And this time, I nail it. Perfect. *(as Huston:)* 'Miss Monroe, the part was already yours.'

(suddenly sad and back in the chair) Johnny's heart gave out just before Christmas 1950. I was with him every day at the hospital. The gossips said I'd worked him too hard. And they'd say it again, with Clark. *(struggles to say 'Bastards', fails and ends up stammering hard, changes tack)* Monsters. His wife tried to keep me from the funeral, but I... I went all the same. I wanted to respect her wishes, but this was Johnny and he wanted me there so I went. They spat at me. Afterwards, I left my car in a note to Natasha. I swallowed all the pills I could find and...

Telephone rings. She turns and looks, weighing something up. She lets it ring twice more before picking up on the stage left side of the bed.

(tetchily) Hello?

The music again, only this time we start to get a distorted sense of the tune.

An act of discretion has her turning her back to the audience.

Don't you have anything better to do? *(no response)* There are people here, you know?

Slams receiver down.

Gee, I'm flaky. *(pause, then sudden manic panic)* Maybe I should go down to the beach?

Quickly picks up receiver, listens, hears nothing and almost immediately dials as she addresses the audience and sits on the stage right edge of the bed.

Natasha found me. After I took the pills, I mean. She got me help. *(beat)* Busy.

Quickly replaces receiver.

Doing this phone business quickly means we negate the need for a much-too-fussy 'engaged tone' sound effect, which just gets in the way.

Great. I wonder if he's there?

Getting groggy and tired now.

Not a day passes that I don't think of Bobby. I mean Johnny.

Suddenly buzzy and glamorous again, she gets up and comes downstage.

When he'd gone, I had to work twice as hard. Fox Dictator Zanuck said I wasn't photogenic. But publicity liked me, so they pushed my cheesecake profile into something he couldn't ignore. My face went global and the mail came in sacks. I was getting more than Grable. Remember that meeting Fox held for its distributors? All the stars came out, and a room full of hot-blooded men swept past them all to get at Sugar here. *(a selection of newspapermen voices:)* 'What's your next picture gonna be?' 'How long do we have to wait?' But there was no film, so I pointed at Zanuck. 'Ask him'.

(proud announcement) Next day, seven-year contract. Five hundred a week, regular raise. Pussy's cock-sucking days are over. *(pause)* Gee, I hope that didn't shock you. You probably imagined the worst anyway. Well, just so you know... There were times – not many, let me say – but times when girls like Pussy here took to their carpet-burned knees and cut deals. Hungry's easy. Life on the wrong side of a movie camera isn't. Pussy

wanted to work and not be kept. Pussy wanted control of her life. Most of those producers were hideous, so Pussy deserved everything she got out of them. And the pleasure was all theirs, believe me. So, yeah. Suddenly Fox is telling the world I'm the most exciting thing in Hollywood. Zanuck doesn't believe it, but the public do. They allow this *(gestures between herself and the audience).*

(animated) Gee, if I hadn't had Natasha... Fox hated me having her on set, but if they hadn't dumped me the first time around... I met her at Columbia. My first real ally in the business. Maybe my last, I don't know. She even got me classes with Michael Chekhov. Expensive, but he *was* Stanislavsky's best student. He said he got 'sex vibrations' when he saw my pictures. Fine, but I wanted to be an actor not an aphrodisiac. With Michael I was Cordelia in *Lear*. With Columbia, I was second billing in a B-picture. Not even close. But the first time I walked past a movie house and... It was a lot to... you know? But there it was. My big name. I walked up and down, just looking at it until it stopped being words. I think I felt sad that it didn't say 'Norma Jeane'. All the people who'd known me as a kid would never know it was me.

Natasha got me through every picture till *Bus Stop*, my first movie after the Actors Studio. *(thinks, heading towards the bedside table to take a pill from the bottle there)* Boy, if she'd been there for my first test... *(swings back to audience and comes downstage, mid-thought)* D'you know how I got that test? Howard Hughes. If he hadn't crashed his plane or whatever it was he crashed, then he wouldn't have been laid up in bed with a pile of *Laff* and *Titter* magazines. I was all over them, smiling out at the world in the hope that someone might notice. *(through gritted glamour model grin)* 'Save me. Please.' Howard owned RKO. Before it died. When Fox heard RKO was interested, they quickly offered me a colour test with Mr Shamroy – one of the best. On a Grable set, too. They had me do this.

She plays the following with a combination of reverence and ironic, amused melodrama. Positions herself at far stage left. Adopts character, pouts melodramatically (dropping character for but an instant she gives the audience a twinkling, knowing wink), turns head to face towards bed, walks across stage, sits on bed, opens compact, smooths eyebrows, pouts, closes compact,

*walks to far stage right, looks out at audience, pouts. Dropping
character, she comes downstage centre, takes a bow.*

Not bad, huh? I added the bow just now, but that's how I got
started. In movies, I mean. Mr Shamroy said *(as Shamroy:)*
'Every frame radiates sex.' If I'd had Natasha back then, we
could've nipped it in the bud. *(sits in chair)* But… standing
blind beneath those lights, with a camera eating up everything
I did… I suddenly knew myself. And that's how Marilyn was
born. *(toasts that notion with glass of water and swigs down a pill
from her pocket)* Fox recommended the name change. 'Monroe',
after my grandmother, and 'Marilyn' for Marilyn Miller – the
Broadway star? I was Norma Jeane Dougherty, before then, but
you knew that, right?

(pauses to think of something else to amaze us with; then:) I worked in
munitions, did you know that? During the war. Spraying plane
parts with banana oil. The glamour! But that's how I got into
modelling. Pictures of working women boosted morale. The
Army took some of me. Nothing glitzy – I shared the cover
of *Family Circle* with a sheep – but it got my face around. I'd
always wanted to be in movies and this seemed like a way in. My
pictures bought me a contract with Miss Snively at Blue Book.

Two days into my first job, they send me home, no explanation.
I'm devastated. Miss Snively says it's because I'm too distracting.
After she moves me into bathing suits, no one ever sends me
home. *(thinks)* Gee, it was Miss Snively that turned me blonde.
(as Miss Snively:) 'It's better for photographers, dear. More
flexible.' We dyed it, cut it short… That was a shock! My
husband hated it. *(realises she hasn't mentioned she was married)*
Yeah, I was married. To Jim. You don't know him.

Jim was older than me. He lived across the way. *(laughing at
herself)* I thought he was intellectual because he liked classical
music. He didn't mind that I was illegitimate. I'd just found
out. That was a surprise. I'd always been told my father died in
an automobile accident. Just after I was born. We got married
just after my sixteenth birthday. June 19th, 1942. I carried the
biggest, whitest bouquet you ever saw. Send me white roses
and I'm yours till the day I die. *(thinks, lost in the memories)*
The minister taught Jim to shoot when he was little. *(thinks)*
I couldn't get that out of my mind all through the ceremony.

(gets out of chair and hurries downstage, conspiratorially) Listen, this is a secret. My biggest worry about marrying Jim was sex. My dear Aunt Ana even bought me a book. For the bride-to-be, y'know? Poor Jim had to help me take out my diaphragm, I was so ignorant. But sex is confusing when... when it doesn't... 'happen'. And it doesn't 'happen' for me as much as I'd like. Jim didn't mind. It always happened for him. But I'd lie on his chest as he fell asleep, wondering if the world was mad, thinking: 'Am I the only one who doesn't get this?' *(thinks)* That whole marriage was a sort of friendship with... privileges. If that's what you want to call them. I guess that's all any marriage is.

(thinks) He shot a deer, once, and put it in the car to bring home, but it woke up, thrashing like a mad thing, screaming. I begged him to let it go, but he just opened the rear door, grabbed its throat and strangled it to death.

(thinks) But he'd hold my hand in the street and snuggle up to me at the movies. When my period was bad, he took care of me. When I traced my father, he stood by me. All the way. I called Mr Gifford long distance and told him I was... I was his daughter. Shaking with nerves and... Jim held me so tightly. It took strength to call a stranger out of the clear blue like that, and... When Gifford hung up without a word, I... Well Jim picked up the pieces.

(walks to the bedside table, to take a pill from the bottle there) When he joined the Merchant Marine... Something changed. *(takes the pill with a swig of water)* Like he didn't trust me or... believe in our marriage the way I did.

She slams the glass down on the table and angrily stomps back downstage.

Truth is, I've never lied to my men about who I am. Joe, Jim, Arthur... But they all invented a character for me. Whether they were falling in or out of love with me... they were loving or lamenting somebody I wasn't.

Jim was in Shanghai when I wrote and told him my plans for getting into movies, I thought he'd have some ideas. I was right. He had a very big idea, called *(as Jim:)* 'Forget it!'. *(thinks)*

If it hadn't been for my dear Aunt Ana, I wouldn't have had anywhere to live.

I wish I could see *her* again. *(sits in the chair)* She was always there, and she didn't have to be, because she wasn't really my aunt. She was Grace's aunt. Grace was my guardian. Aunt Ana lived alone and had space, so... We lived in the upstairs half of a house. It was a poor neighbourhood and she let the downstairs to another family. *(thinks)* I was a county child, did you know that? *(challenging and cold)* Do you know *anything* about me? The *real me?* Before *her.* I was an orphan. We'd queue for hours to buy twenty-five cent sacks of stale bread – like Melba Toasts, y'know? – but it had to last a week. *(thinks)* I've had some high times the last ten years, but... Living with my Aunt Ana... That was the happiest time of my life. *(sudden moment of clarity)* Wow. I don't think I got that... till now. I loved that woman... When the girls at school teased the way I dressed, she could see I was hurt. *(as Ana:)* 'These things don't matter, Norma Jeane. It's who you are that counts. You just get on and be yourself, honey.' I wanted to stay with her – for ever – but she was old and sick and... If anything happened to her, I'd be sent back to the orphanage. Grace wanted to make sure I'd be okay, so... Enter Jim! The best she could do was marry me off. Typical Grace. She had my interests at heart, but...

(thinks) When I was a little girl and my mother got ill, there was... *(chooses words carefully)* Well, there was all kinds of... stuff... I went through. Difficult stuff. So I was sent to live with Grace, who was living with a guy named Doc. Mr Big Movie Star. He wasn't. He was too lazy for that. He always looked at me funny. Yeah. So... A month after their wedding, I was living in an orphanage. That's Grace.

(gets up from chair) I felt so betrayed, I cried for weeks. Me, an orphan? My mother's still alive! Locked away for a crime I didn't commit. Sentenced to blend, unnoticed, in that hateful uniform. *(thinks)* But in the school shower – amongst the non-orphanage girls who wore clothes I could only dream of – I was free. Naked, I was just like them. I even had the edge. In those showers I willed myself to develop... and I did. Real quick. *(she sits on the end of the bed)* When my first period came, it sliced through me like a hot poker. No change there. It just about

knocked me out, but now I was a woman. And those girls knew it.

She idly picks up the compact mirror from the bed, touching her cheeks and pouting a bit; not over-exaggerated, just her 'mirror face'.

I'd curl my hair... maybe powder my nose, which was growing like Pinocchio. *(prods and plays with her nose, dissatisfied)* Lumpy, bumpy, puppet nose. I spend hours getting my face right. It takes time to become Marilyn Monroe... to lose the tension and the sadness. The broken capillaries, the disappointed mouth. Most of my time goes on this thing. *(her nose)* That and my dead eyes. My mother's eyes. *(pulls at skin under one eye)* I'm getting old. I don't want to get old. *(puts compact down on bed)*

(sudden animation again) My earliest memories aren't of my own mother, but of Mrs Ida. And Daddy Wayne. Growing vegetables, raising chickens, goats... other people's kids. The house was full of kids. Their own and foster-kids like me. And if we were naughty – whack! – the razor strap. *(gets up from bed)* I thought it might help if I called them 'Ma' and 'Pa' – like the other kids did – but they put me straight on that. *(as Ida:)* 'That woman who comes weekends – she's your Ma.' 'Ma' was the pretty lady that couldn't smile. The lady with the sunset hair. The sad lady. Gladys, they called her. *(walks to the bedside table to take a pill)* It must've been tough. Boarding me out like that. But times were hard and she had two mouths to feed. So I went to Hawthorne with Ida and Wayne. *(takes a pill from the bottle on or by the table, with water)* Five dollars a week, plus extra for piano lessons. My grandmother lived across the street.

(standing in the lamplight) Della Monroe. They say she was a beauty in her time, but she had *moods*. One day she rescued me from Ida's razor strap by breaking down the door and carrying me home. I remember waking up in this dark room and... this old woman, up real close. She pushed something onto my face – maybe a pillow. I felt such a terrifying breathlessness. I was too young to resist, so I don't know why she stopped. The police dragged her off to Norwalk – the insane hospital – where her heart seized up. And that was the end of Della Monroe. *(thinks)* But wherever I go, she comes with me. And not just her name. Whenever I go to bed without pills, I feel what that baby girl

felt. That panic. I'm afraid to sleep... in case... in case I never wake up. As if the dark could stifle every breath.

(with great, shambolic energy she comes downstage) Turns out, Ida and Wayne *offered* to adopt, but Mother said no. She could only see me at weekends – and then not every weekend – because her hours were long and so was the tram-ride. *(thinks)* She'd mumble. To herself. Prayers and psalms, I think. I knew what sadness was, but Momma's sadness seemed so vast, so... black. On bad days she'd just cry and I'd beg her to stop. But on good days... I remember eating ice cream on the beach, watching jugglers and fire-eaters and listening to the curling smash of the ocean... And when I had whooping cough, she brought me back to Hollywood to take care of me. Do you know how happy she made me? I was finally at the centre of someone's attention.

Hollywood should've been glamorous, but Mother's room was basic. The only thing that stood out was the picture on the wall. A man in a slouch hat. Black hair, thin moustache... I liked his face so I asked who he was. *(as Mother:)* 'That's your father'. I can't describe the... electric thrill that ran through me. Every moment I could, I stared into his face. My very own daddy, who would rescue me from my sadness. I'd hold my breath and tense my body, afraid that Mother would make me stop. But Mother just turned and said, *(as Mother:)* 'He's not coming, Norma Jeane. He's dead.'

(her energy increasing, becoming gradually manic) A few years later, she bought us a bungalow, and I said goodbye to Ida and Wayne. We lived in two rooms and Mother let the rest to an acting couple from England. It was a whole new life... a whole new world. I guess what makes me different to most movie people I meet is that I was a Hollywood kid. Mother would take me to Grauman's and show me the hands and feet. Grauman's was a pretty cheap baby-sitter. I'd sit there all day, right up in front. Whatever they showed, I loved... Charles Laughton – now there's a man... *(wryly, squeezing an imaginary breast)* Joan Crawford. *(excited)* And I *loved* Jean Harlow. We all did. *(even more excited)* And Clark! With his black hair and his thin moustache. I even wondered if he might be the man in Mother's special picture. Yeah, I told myself. He just might be

at that. *(really excited)* Suddenly, shy little Noodle was telling any kid who'd listen that her daddy was a movie star.

(sudden shift into dark introspection) Mother always had a smile, but she was sad. I thought it was me, but bills, pills and Jesus had the edge. One day, I came home from school, to be greeted by the acting couple from England. *(laughing again now, a drunken, groggy giddiness that masks her childhood terror)* Gently, kindly, they told me that Mother had gone to hospital for a little rest. Overwhelmed by emptiness, she'd called in sick. They found her trembling under the stairs, hysterical... inconsolable. The ambulance, took her – screaming and laughing – to Norwalk... where Grandma Della had died. She was a broken ghost.

She's laughing, but only gently now and it's obvious she's not sure why. It gradually fades from her – but by no means quickly – to be replaced by still contemplation, in front of the now darkened white hanging. She takes a long moment to steel herself, taking in each individual audience member in silence; all of them, for however long it takes.

The following sequence is played out in stillness, the stage is now mostly dark, so only her face is lit to any great extent. All physical movement below the neck is halted or minimal for now, except where noted.

I was eight when... Gladys... my mother... got too ill to look after me. She allowed Grace to be my guardian. But until the legal stuff was sewn up, I was fostered again. This didn't last long. *(pause)* Because of Kimmel. *(thinks)* Kimmel was... Kimmel was the jolly old man who rented the room at the top of the house I was fostered in. He was the heart of the house, and – I'll guess – the heart of its income. Everyone loved him, or pretended they did... Really, though, he... He wasn't so old. I guess he just seemed that way to an eight-year-old girl. The day I met him, he gave me a nickel, for ice cream... So I'd follow him around, hoping he'd do it again.

Telephone rings. She looks at it annoyed, perhaps, and then defiant, as she lets it ring. It rings three more times then stops. Satisfied, she continues her story.

One day I'm sent upstairs with towels for the closet near his room. He waves from his open door, in his vest and pants. His face is red and framed with soap from shaving. He asks for a towel and beckons me in. He says he has something for me. Hoping for another nickel, I walk in. I hand him the towel and... He bolts the door. I see him do it but don't realise what it means. He... He sits me on the bed... he's going to show me something... something special. Like a magician, he finds a nickel in my ear. He holds it out... for me to take – a whole nickel! – but when I reach out he snatches it away. 'Ah-ah,' he says, sitting beside me. 'How about a kiss first?' *(thinks)* So I kiss him. A peck, on the cheek. I'm a little girl. Old men are always asking little girls to do this stuff... to perform. 'Not bad,' he says. And then he tells me I'll have to try harder. He tells me to sit on his lap, and I do, thinking nothing of it. Then *he* kisses *me*. I mean, *kisses* me. His hot, wide head presses, roughly, on my little face, his slimy, salty tongue, pushes... into my mouth. He smells of soap, of sweat, of disease, of death. *(beat)* He smells of soap. I pull away, choking and sobbing, but he just shushes me, waving the nickel... Like it's a prize I can't afford to lose by drawing attention to... to what's going on. *(as Kimmel:)* 'It's only a game.' Then he pushes me back, onto the bed, covering my crying mouth with a fat hand and climbing into my panties with the other. He touches me, and he's so calm that I realise I'm shaking. My vision blurs and I... My mind turns itself off. I might never move or speak again. I've left my rag doll body and floated up to the brown-stained ceiling. Pressing my face into the plaster so I won't have to look down and see what Kimmel's doing to that empty little girl on the bed. I think I hear him speak... I think I hear the whispers that he grunts into her deaf ears... He's breathing fast and hard as he tells her she's beautiful. And she is. *(voice breaking)* She's so beautiful. *(pause)* She's never been so beautiful. Then, in angry, strangled tones, he tells her she's disgusting and she deserves no better. And with a tight, exploding cry... a breathless whimper... a croaking, rasping gurgle that fills her empty world, he's done. The tiny silence that follows stretches, unhindered, into the future. To this room, here, now, today, tonight. Tomorrow. Then he stands and tells her to 'Get out!' He doesn't even look at her. Just unbolts the door and strides off to the bathroom. The little girl and me are... reunited... by a sudden sense of

loss and despair that... even... twenty-eight years later I have
no hope of expressing. And... When I'm able to stand,
there's... a pain I've never known before. A pain that'll curse
me for the rest of my life. And suddenly I'm made of tears,
running downstairs in search of someone... someone to tell...
someone to help me... *(pause)* My foster-mother screams at me
for making 'evil accusations' about 'that nice man'. She drags
me back upstairs and tells him what I've said. He pretends he's
shocked...dismayed. If he made me do such things for a nickel,
then where's the nickel? I have no nickel. I have nothing.
'There you go,' he yells, and throws the nickel at me. I want to
say something, but I can't... can't, I...

*Struggles to get this out, face contorting, mouth reaching
desperately for words. And it is here that the telephone rings again.
She ignores it and continues with her story, raising her voice and
fighting to be heard over the insistent ringing.*

I can't get my words out. *(overcompensating with each word to
prevent her stammer)* Not... one... emerges... unbroken. *(as
foster-mother:)* 'Don't do that, Norma Jeane. Don't stutter.'
(overcompensating again to fend off stammer) I'm... slapped...
in the mouth and... thrown... into my room. Sent to... hell
to... burn... with bad people. Punished and... whipped with...
a cloth, a wet cloth on... The bad part of my body, she says.
I feel... like... I feel like dying, but I don't know how to make
it happen. If only I could, I...

*Annoyed, turns to grabs the receiver – from stage right side of the
bed – succeeding exactly the moment the person on the other end
hangs up. We hear the 'dead' tone. She holds the receiver limply,
then replaces it. She's enveloped by deep sadness. Something lost,
long ago.*

I was a stupid kid.

*She covers her face with both hands, lowers head for a moment,
then emerges, cheerful and energised, almost glamourous – her
genuine self. She comes downstage.*

(takes a dry pill from the bottle in her pocket) Mother's little 'rest'
turned out to be not-so little. It was eleven years before we were
back under the same roof. But she was a stranger. I didn't know

how to deal with her. We shared a bed and she'd hold me in the moonlight like *I was her mother* and not the other way around. And the money I made didn't cover us both. I had to make ends meet, so… Well, I got into situations a person doesn't feel good talking about. To keep Mother in good clothes, I… I sank so low, I… Well, without that first Fox contract, I don't know how I'd have clawed my way back.

When I left, she lost herself in Jesus and asked the hospital to take her back. *(a sudden flash of steel to counter any criticism)* But her bills are covered. They always will be. *(sits on the end of the bed)* Was it selfish? Maybe. But I was offered a whole bunch of opportunities that wouldn't come again. *(pause)* I was on contract, I had money, I could buy clothes, provide for my mother… Better than being the girl they find in the unmade bed. The sleeping pill suicide. With her infantile mother clinging like cobwebs to her frozen, blue body.

(drowsily and drunkenly) And I have you to thank for that. *(at audience)* You. So, thank you. But I know now how… insubstantial this is… *(gestures expansively about stage and auditorium)* You create envy, you see. In people you don't even know. People who walk up to me and say wonderful things, lovely things… cruel things… disgusting things. Like it won't hurt me. Like it's only happening to the bleach in my hair or the mascara round my eyes. *(thinks)* I used to think that if I could do it all again, I'd do it differently. *(joking)* 'If I could live my life over, I'd live over a saloon'. I'd think of Mother and it'd hurt a hundred times more than it did when I was little. I do what I can, but… I haven't always done enough. And that's the part that hurts the most. But even if I unpicked my life, in all directions, and got rid of the bad stuff… the orphanage and Kimmel and the miscarriages… Well, it wouldn't matter if I lost *you*… but to never have had dear Aunt Ana, or Claude and Hedda; Johnny or Joe? Bobby even. Never to have found what I found tonight? No. *(thinks)* I'm not a scared little girl any more.

That's the last point at which we see her face, because she's turned, grabbing the compact mirror, to tiredly crawl along the bed to make her way into her final position; the position in which she began the play.

I'll take the remarkable life I've had, thank you, and keep on moving. Accept the past and be brave enough to set the bad parts free. Because life starts now. Right now. There may not be a man in my life, but finally… *(now slumped into her final position, on her tummy, facing away from us, legs up in the air, crossed, behind her)* finally, I've got someone special. Someone I know I can love if I try hard enough. The only person who ever stood by me, through good and bad. Me. Finally me. My own truth. If I went through all that to find myself… then… I guess it was worth it. *(picks up the compact mirror and looks at herself, face turned away from us; no pout, no pose, just herself)* What have you got to be proud of, Marilyn Monroe? *(she smiles and drops the arm holding the compact mirror)* Everything. Everything.

Telephone rings. She laughs and lazily reaches her left arm out to pick up the receiver. We can hear the tinny music getting louder before she does. The louder it gets, the brighter the light gets on stage.

Oh, it's you. Persistent. Kept you waiting, huh? *(laughs)*

Music getting louder, light getting brighter, but she's too content and stoned to be scared.

Okay, I'm done now. *(half into telephone, half at audience, dropping her receiver arm and snuggling into the bed, face down, face turned away from us)* Good night, sleep tight… sweet repose. Wherever you lay your head… I hope you find your nose. *(laughs, happily)*

Assumes final/opening position.

(to herself) Maybe I should go down to the beach?

Music builds until we can clearly hear Marilyn Monroe singing I Wanna Be Loved By You *all across the stage.*

Her 'crossed' legs finally, but slowly, drunkenly, drop.

She is still. Dead still.

The light is painful to look at.

Blackout.

PROPERTY LIST

Set

Single divan bed, unmade: white sheet, two thin white pillows, silver shiny comforter. Angled so the foot of the bed is toward the audience, downstage centre, the head of the bed, upstage right.

Small modern chrome and glass bedside table/nightstand.

Practical and sturdy period bedside lamp, on bedside table.

Cigarette case in silver with cigarettes, on bedside table.

Period modern clock, with hands, on bedside table (set to and stopped at 11.55).

Small glass of water by bedside table.

Large, used ashtray by bedside table.

Small bedroom chair, maybe Lloyd Loom style, white; far downstage stage left.

Women's' worn clothes, underwear, headscarves and some sour towels, around bed and on chair (see *Notes for a Production* for item and colour suggestions).

Small glass of water by the chair, with small decanter, possibly coloured glass.

Several small practical pill bottles – white plastic and brown glass – all labelled by pharmacy on table and on floor beneath, also by chair.

A four-foot wide vertical hanging of white gauze, suggestive of a French window, but also to be used as a backdrop to both the Trans-Lux and 'rape' sequences, just off the centre of the stage, upstage left.

Cosmetic items, on table – including pot of *Nivea* face cream.

A white early 1960s US style telephone on the bed. Practical.

A 1950s/1960s gold compact mirror on the bed.

Prominent piles of displaced items: books/record albums/ photos/handbags/framed pictures – not too much, but all chaotic and without structure or design. Department store shopping bags (plain brown or white paper is fine, but also *Bloomingdales* or *Jax*) being used as storage: full of clothes, shoes, etc.

Several piles of books (see *Notes for a Production* for which books).

Small pile of vinyl record albums (see *Notes for a Production* for which artists).

Small framed photo representing Joe DiMaggio's son.

Small framed photo representing Arthur Miller's son and daughter.

Large, very visible framed picture of Abraham Lincoln.

Very bright red A5 size diary, discarded, partly under bed but noticeable.

Shoes.

Pair of weathered fluffy slippers, not necessarily next to each other.

Chanel No 5 and/or *Arpege* bottle/s – sprayed around the set before performance and worn by the performer.

Scattered used tissues, stained.

Personal

Practical pill bottles (two differing kinds, each with its own distinct type of easily edible pill) in pocket of Noodle's dressing gown.

Practical sticks of gum in pocket of Noodle's dressing gown.

Some crumpled tissues in pocket of Noodle's dressing gown.

LIGHTING PLOT

Practical fittings required: practical bedside table lamp.

Interior. Natural light from 'outside' (8pm, California) that gradually gets darker in 'real time' over course of play, until descended into almost total gloom by the end.

The second half (from Page 17) is lit by a practical table lamp (supported by stage lighting), but 'outside' it continues to get darker.

To open: General interior lighting, already beginning approx. 40 min fade to almost total darkness

Cue 1: 'In the end it was a skirt that pushed   (Page 18) us apart…'

Fade up spotlight on Noodle from head to ankles

Cue 2: '…that my marriage must end.'   (Page 19)

Fade down spot on Noodle.

Cue 3: Noodle reaches to switch on practical   (Page 19) lamp.

Bring in supporting lights for lamplight effect, stage right.

Cue 4: 'She was a broken ghost.'   (Page 29)

Fade up tight, dark, spot on Noodle from shoulders up.

Cut supporting lights for lamp.

Cue 5: Noodle grabs the ringing phone.   (Page 33)

Cut tight, dark spot and restore lamp support lights.

Cue 6:   'Everything. Everything.'   (Page 33)

Lights gradually building in blinding intensity until play ends.

Cue 7:   Noodle's legs drop to bed and she is   (Page 33)
still.

Cut audience blinders with sudden blackout.

EFFECTS PLOT

Cue 1: On lights-up from pre-set (Page 1)

1960s US telephone ring x 4

Cue 2: 'Who is this? Pete?' (Page 1)

Static-heavy distorted recording of Marilyn Monroe song I Wanna Be Loved by You *– the audience should be barely able to hear it let alone discern what it is*

Cue 3: Noodle slams phone receiver into its cradle (Page 1)

Cut I Wanna Be Loved by You *cue*

Cue 4: 'So I took an overdose and killed myself.' (Page 8)

1960s US telephone ring x 2

Cue 5: Four-Seven-Six-One-Eight-Nine-Oh. (Page 8)

Slightly less static-heavy distorted recording of Marilyn Monroe song I Wanna Be Loved by You *than before – but the audience can still barely hear it or discern what it is*

Cue 6: Noodle slams phone receiver into its cradle (Page 8)

Cut I Wanna Be Loved by You *cue*

Cue 7: 'I swallowed all the pills I could find and...' (Page 21)

1960s US telephone ring x 3

Cue 8: She picks up telephone receiver. (Page 21)

Slightly less static-heavy distorted recording of Marilyn Monroe song I Wanna Be Loved by You *than last time – the audience can now just sense that there might be a tune, but not what that tune actually is*

Cue 9:   Noodle slams phone receiver into its   (Page 21)
cradle

Cut I Wanna Be Loved by You *cue*

Cue 10:   '…hoping he'd do it again.'   (Page 29)

1960s US telephone ring x 4

Cue 11:   '…but I can't…can't, I…'   (Page 31)

1960s US telephone ring (continual)

Cue 12:   She snatches up telephone receiver.   (Page 31)

Cut 1960s US telephone ring (continual)

Replace with: Telephone dead tone

Cue 13:   She replaces telephone receiver.   (Page 31)

Cut telephone dead tone

Cue 14:   'Everything. Everything.'   (Page 33)

1960s US telephone ring x 2

Cue 15:   She picks up telephone receiver.   (Page 33)

Slightly less static-heavy distorted recording of Marilyn Monroe song I Wanna Be Loved by You *than last time – as the scene unfolds to the end of the play, the music becomes less distorted, gradually filling the stage, achieving full audio clarity on the line about not being able to aspire to anything higher (approx. 2m.24s) as Noodle's legs begin to drop to the bed.*

NB. A helpful hint. This can all be timed carefully – as in the original production – so that once Noodle's legs have finally dropped and she is lying still, the song has reached the breathy 'pooooh!' of Monroe blowing a kiss (approx. 2m.40s), which is, as you'll observe, a rather smart cue for the lighting blackout.

Lightning Source UK Ltd.
Milton Keynes UK
UKOW06f1824170116

266569UK00014B/380/P